PLAYERS IN PIGTAILS

TAKE ME OUT TO THE BALL GAME

Katie Casey was baseball mad.
Had the fever and had it bad;
Just to root for the hometown crew,
Every sou Katie blew.
On a Saturday her young beau
Called to see if she'd like to go
To see a show, but Miss Kate said . . .
"No, I'll tell you what you can do.

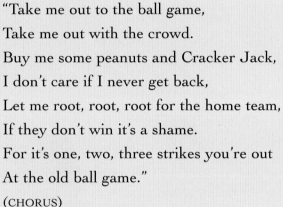

"Take me out to the ball game,
Take me out with the crowd.
Buy me some peanuts and Cracker Jack,
I don't care if I never get back,
Let me root, root, root for the home team,
If they don't win it's a shame.
For it's one, two, three strikes you're out
At the old ball game."
(CHORUS)

Katie Casey saw all the games,
Knew the players by their full names;
Told the umpire he was wrong,
All along, good and strong.
When the score was just two to two,
Katie Casey knew what to do,
Just to cheer up the boys she knew,
She made the gang sing this song:
(REPEAT CHORUS)

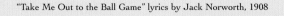

"Take Me Out to the Ball Game" lyrics by Jack Norworth, 1908

PLAYERS IN

PIGTAILS

BY SHANA COREY

ILLUSTRATED BY

REBECCA GIBBON

SCHOLASTIC INC.

NEW YORK   TORONTO   LONDON   AUCKLAND   SYDNEY
MEXICO CITY   NEW DELHI   HONG KONG   BUENOS AIRES

acknowledgments The author would like to acknowledge the following for making this book possible. The many wonderful books about the league: *Belles of the Ballpark* by Diana Star Helmer, *A Whole New Ball Game: The Story of the All-American Girls Professional Baseball League* and *Winning Ways: The History of American Women in Sports* by Sue Macy, *Women at Play: The Story of Women in Baseball* by Barbara Gregorich, and *Women in Baseball: The Forgotten History* by Gai Ingham Berlage. The All-American Girls Professional Baseball League Players' Association, Inc. and their Web site (www.aagpbl.org). The inspiring motion picture *A League of Their Own.* My friends at Scholastic—Marijka Kostiw, Leslie Budnick, and especially and always Tracy Mack. And above all, my dad, for too many reasons to count, among them his patient explanation of baseball over the telephone (long distance, of course). CRACKER JACK is a registered trademark of Recot, Inc.

Katie Casey wasn't good at being a girl . . .

. . . at least not the kind of girl

everyone thought she should be.

Her clothing was crumpled.

Her knitting was knotted.

Her dancing was a disaster.

FUND-
RAISING
DANCE
FOR THE
WAR EFFORT
FRIDAY -
NOVEMBER 6th
1942

And no matter how hard she tried,

her heart just wasn't in home ec.

But there was one thing Katie *was* good at.

BASEBALL.

Katie could catch any ball with any mitt with her eyes closed.

She could hit any ball with any bat with one hand behind her back.

She preferred sliding to sewing, batting to baking, and

home runs to homecoming.

Her parents were not at all pleased.

"Why not piano or painting?" they pleaded.

"What good is baseball to a girl?"

But Katie wouldn't be swayed.

She walked baseball. She talked baseball.

She even dreamed baseball.

She went to the ballpark every chance she got.

She loved the hot dogs and peanuts.

She loved the shouting and singing.

But most of all she loved watching the professional players play ball.

Sometimes, she even imagined she was one of them.

Every spring she showed up for Fairfield High team tryouts.

And every spring she was turned away without even getting a try.

"Better stick to ballet," the boys said.

"What good is baseball to a girl?"

But baseball was starting to change.

America was at war, and more and more

of the country's boys—including the professional

baseball players—were going off to fight.

The fields were almost empty,

and the fans were getting frantic.

Even President Roosevelt was worried.

What was a country

without a national pastime?

No one wanted to find out.

Finally, Phillip Wrigley, the owner of the Chicago Cubs, had an idea.

"If women can work in factories and even join the army," he said,

"why can't they play ball?"

"**OUTRAGEOUS!**" everyone said.

"Girls playing baseball?

No one will pay to see girls play ball!"

But Mr. Wrigley didn't listen.

He sent out thirty scouts to find players

for his league—the first and only girls

professional baseball league.

The scouts searched high and low,

near and far, and to be perfectly frank,

they were flabbergasted by what they found.

Washington

All over the country,
girls were playing ball.
And they were playing
just as good as boys.

Texas

California

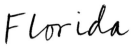
Florida

Louisiana

New York

One of them was Katie Casey.
"Say, sister," said a scout
when he saw her curveball.
"How'd you like to go
to Chicago to try out
for a real team?"

WOULD SHe?!

Katie didn't have to think twice.

She went straight home and packed her bags,

kissed her parents good-bye, and boarded the very next train.

When she got to Wrigley Field,

she broke into a grin.

There were hundreds of girls!

There were farm girls and city girls, tall girls and short girls, girls from far away and girls from down the block. But no matter what they looked like or where they came from, they all had one thing in common.

THEY ALL LOVED BASEBALL.

Katie had never felt so at home.

"Sign her up!" said the coach of the Kenosha Comets when he saw her swing.

The All-American Girls Professional Baseball League was on its way!

Everyone was curious about the strange happenings at Wrigley Field.

"Unheard of!" said one concerned citizen. "Girls don't like sports."

"It's certainly not ladylike," agreed another.

"WHAT GOOD IS BASEBALL TO A GIRL?"

blared the newspaper headlines.

The league managers heard the talk,

and their stomachs started to twitch.

They knew their girls were ready to play ball,

but maybe the country wasn't quite ready

for their girls.

The managers decided to launch an emergency campaign

to show the country just how ladylike baseball could be.

First they designed special uniforms for the girls to wear.

"Dresses?" asked Katie, but she shrugged and put one on.

After all, at least she was getting to play ball.

Then the managers signed the teams up for charm school.

"Pinkies out, girls! Posture!" cried the teacher. "Think swans!"

Finally, it was time for the big test.

The girls were graceful, they were elegant, they were perfectly charming.

And they were ready to **PLAY BALL.**

On opening day, sixteen swanlike players emerged

from each locker room and onto the field.

But something wasn't right.

Katie heard a giggling in the stands. It grew louder and louder.

"Careful, you might break a nail, girls!" someone shouted.

"Players in pigtails?" roared the crowd. "Is this a ballpark or a ballroom?"

Everyone laughed themselves silly, until . . .

. . . the All-American Girls Professional Baseball League started to play. And they played, by far, the best ball any of them had ever played. By the bottom of the ninth, the score was Rockford Peaches, 9, Kenosha Comets, 6. The bases were loaded and Katie Casey was at bat for the Comets.

She stepped up to the plate and looked out at the stands.

She'd been waiting her whole life for this.

The pitcher threw the ball, and Katie swung. . . . CRACK!

The ball sailed up, up, up into the air. Katie took off running.

"It's a grand-slam home run!" shouted the announcer.

The crowd went wild! And Katie cheered right along with them

because for once, no one was asking what good baseball was to a girl.

They were all too busy talking about how good **GiRLS** were for baseball.

AUTHOR'S NOTE Several years ago, I saw the movie *A League of Their Own*, about the All-American Girls Professional Baseball League (AAGPBL). When the movie was over, I couldn't quite leave the subject behind. Was it all true? I wondered, and why didn't I know about it until now?

I did some research, and came across the lyrics to the song "Take Me Out to the Ball Game." In the very first verse were the words "Katie Casey was baseball mad." I couldn't believe it! The song that is synonymous with baseball is about a girl! Now I had two things I couldn't get off my mind.

And so, I decided to write this story using the baseball-loving character Katie Casey as a representative of the many different young women who played in the AAGPBL. While Katie and the game she plays in are fictional, everything else about the league and its history is true.

The league was born during a unique time in America's history. With so many men off fighting in World War II, women were going to work in record numbers: women in the armed forces were fighting for freedom, and female factory workers—symbolized by Rosie the Riveter—were showing the world that woman power was just as valuable as man power.

Phillip Wrigley (owner of the Chicago Cubs and president of the Wrigley chewing gum company) took these cues and, spurred by President Roosevelt's mandate to keep baseball alive, decided to start a professional girls

baseball league. He called it the All-American Girls Softball League and devised a game that was a cross between softball and baseball. As the league evolved, the game became closer to men's baseball. The distance between the bases and pitcher's mounds lengthened, overhand and sidearm pitching replaced underhand pitching, and the 12-inch ball shrunk to Major League Baseball's standard 9¼ inches. And the league's name changed to the All-American Girls Professional Baseball League.

Wrigley's initial plan was for the league to play in Major League stadiums, but when those owners refused, he turned to smaller cities in the Midwest. While Wrigley finalized plans, his scouts fanned out across the United States and Canada searching amateur softball leagues and holding regional tryouts. Everywhere the scouts went they found women who had grown up playing ball with their fathers and brothers or were the stars of their neighborhood pickup games.

In the spring of 1943, hundreds of women and girls came to Chicago for tryouts. After the final cuts, 4 teams were formed: the Rockford Peaches in Illinois, the Racine Belles in Wisconsin, the Kenosha Comets in Wisconsin, and the South Bend Blue Sox in Indiana. Players ranged in age from 15 to 28 years old, and most of them were single, though a few were married with children. The league was not integrated.

Once the teams were selected, Wrigley's primary concern was the league's image. During this time, many people thought sports were a masculine activity and that women who played them were unfeminine. In order to get the public's support for his league, Wrigley wanted to show that being an athlete and being a lady were not mutually exclusive. He had special uniforms designed, made up of short, one-piece dresses over satin panties. But the uniforms weren't exactly suited for playing ball. The players got scrapes and bruises from sliding on bare legs, and sometimes snagged their skirts while winding up to pitch. Still, they looked ladylike so Wrigley kept them.

Wrigley also sent the teams to charm school during spring training. There they were given lessons in how to walk and talk, how to apply makeup, and even what type of clothes to wear. Players also followed strict rules of conduct. They were required to keep their hair well groomed at all times and to always wear lipstick in public —even on the playing field! They had chaperones who enforced curfews and approved where they could eat and what they could do socially.

Despite all this, for most of the players it was worth it. Salaries started at about $45 a week, and star players could earn much more. The players were also traveling—some for the first time— and most importantly, they were getting to play professional baseball!

The league played its first season in the summer of 1943, with games every day and twice on Sundays. Unlike men's professional baseball, the league, and not the individual teams, owned the players' contracts, and Wrigley assigned players so that the level of skill was matched as evenly as possible between teams. This policy led to some of the most exciting games fans had ever seen—in any league!

Patriotism was another part of the league's appeal. Teams held benefit games for the Women's Army Corp and the Red Cross, and each game started with the players lining up in a V for *victory* during "The Star Spangled Banner."

The league was so successful that by 1948, it had expanded from 4 teams to 10. Attendance was high, home cities held parades in their teams' honor, and players became local celebrities.

But by the late 1940s and early 1950s, society was once again shifting. Women were encouraged to leave the factories and the ballparks to make room for returning soldiers. Television was also sweeping the country, eclipsing other forms of entertainment. The crowds at the ballparks dwindled, and after 12 seasons, the AAGPBL folded in 1954.

The league lives on, though, in books, in movies, in the spirit of women and girls who play ball today, and in the hearts and memories of the pioneering women who played in the first-ever All-American Girls Professional Baseball League. This book is a tribute to those women, for knowing that sometimes rooting for the home team just isn't enough, and for having the courage to step up to the plate and PLay BaLL!

VICTORY SONG

Batter up! Hear that call!
The time has come for one and all
To play ball. For we're the members of the All-American League,
We come from cities near and far.
We've got Canadians, Irishmen, and Swedes,
We're all for one, we're one for all,
We're All-American.

Each girl stands, her head so proudly high,
Her motto Do Or Die.
She's not the one to use or need an alibi.
Our chaperones are not too soft,
They're not too tough,
Our managers are on the ball.
We've got a president who really knows his stuff,
We're all for one, we're one for all,
We're All-Americans!

"Victory Song" of the All-American Girls Professional Baseball League was
cowritten by La Vonne "Pepper" Paire-Davis and Nalda "Bird" Phillips, 1944.
Used by permission.